Please do not delet

D1766191

t

HAR

Please renew or return items by the date shown on your receipt

www.hertsdirect.org/libraries

Renewals and enquiries: 0300 123 4049

Textphone for hearing or speech impaired users: 0300 123 4041

L32

London

Hertfordshire

46 808 803 0

4

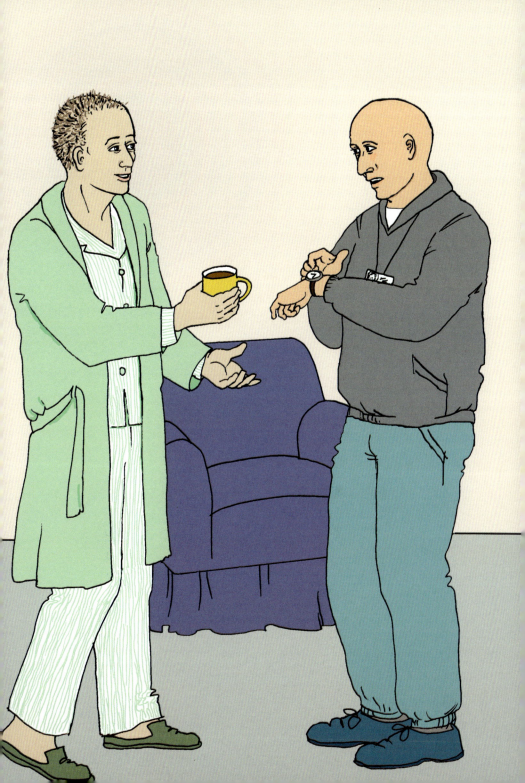

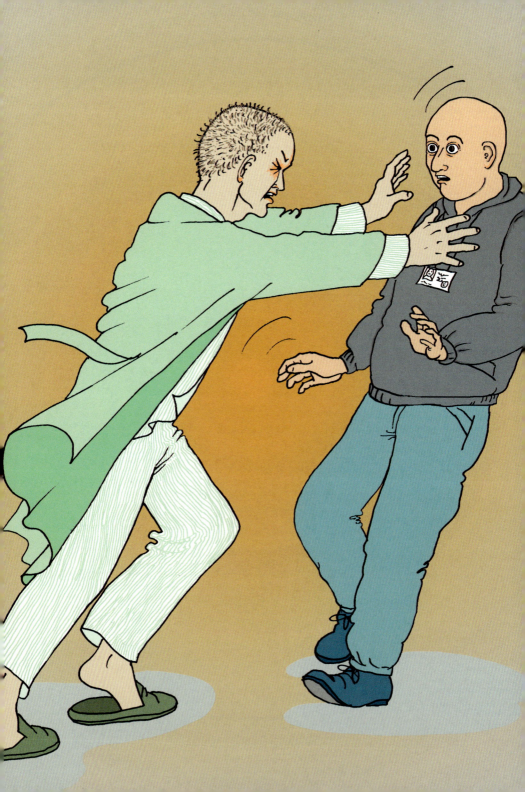

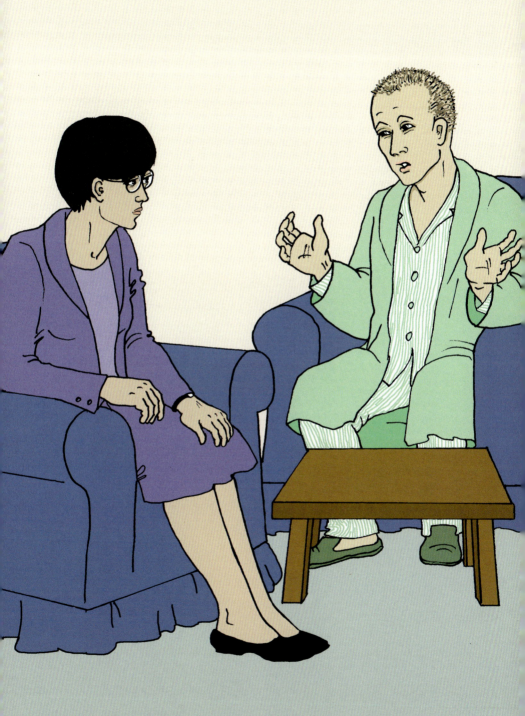

21

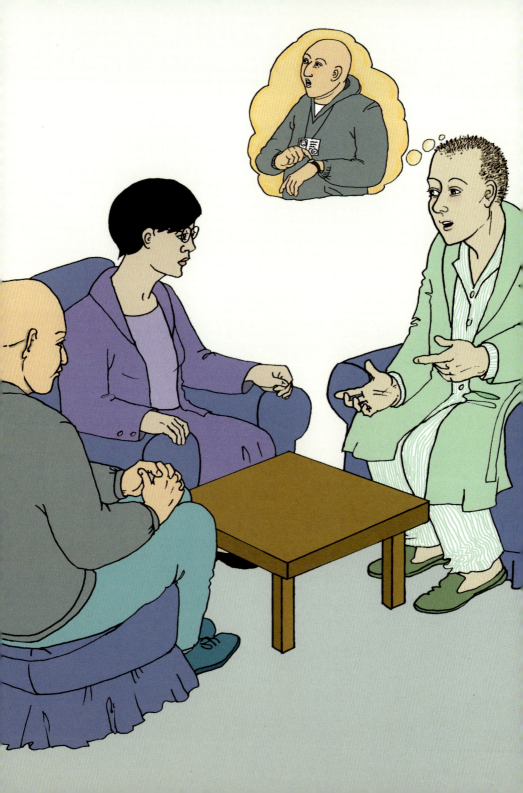

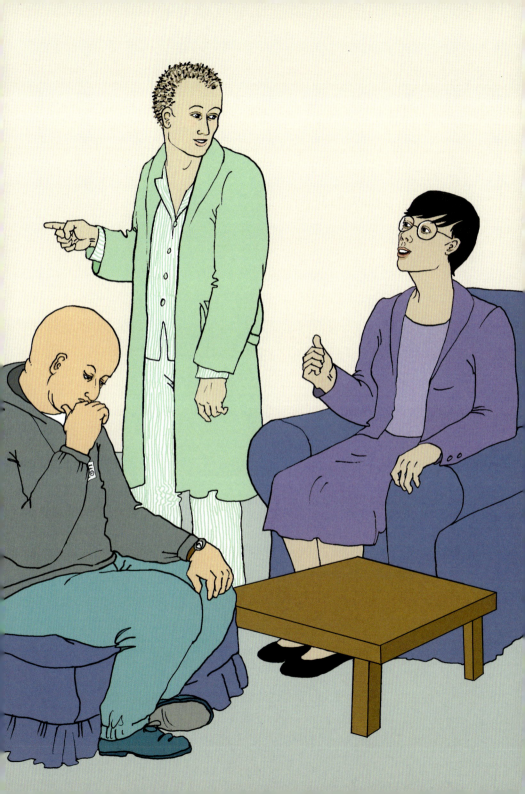

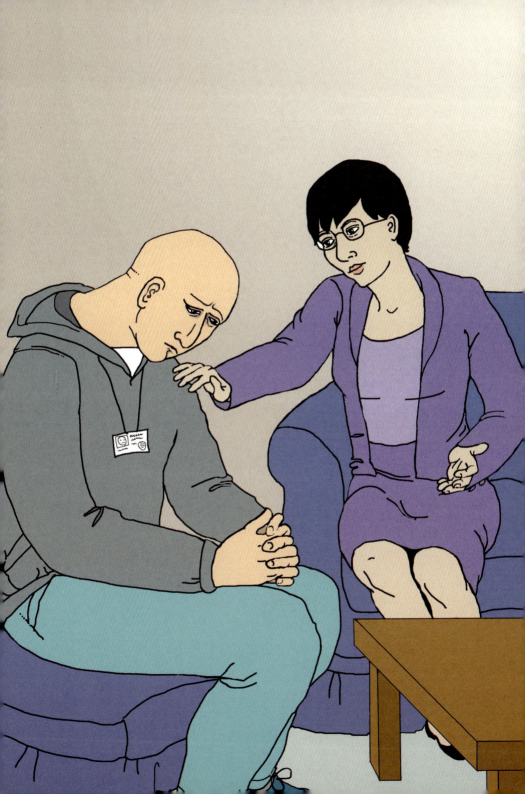

31

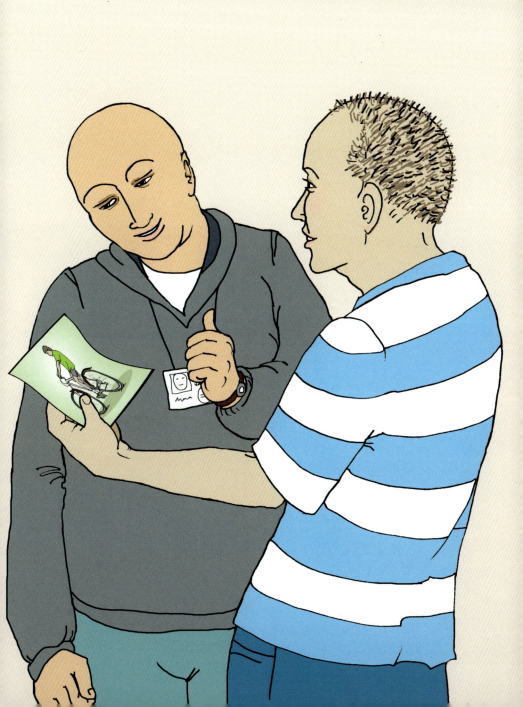

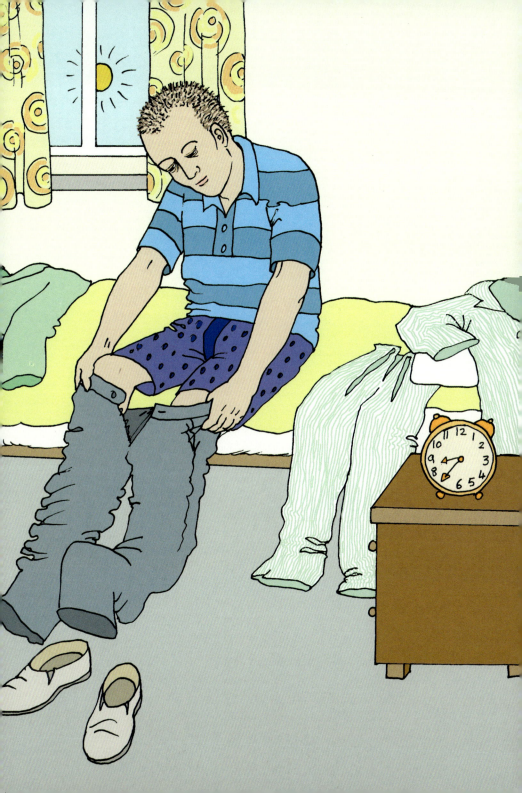

First edition published 2014 by Books Beyond Words.

Text & illustrations © Books Beyond Words 2014.

No part of this book may be reproduced in any form, or by any means without prior permission in writing from the publisher.

ISBN 978-1-78458-029-2

British Library Cataloguing-in-Publication Data
A catalogue record for this book is available from the British Library.

Printed by Advent Print Group, Andover.

Books Beyond Words is a Community Interest Company registered in England and Wales (7557861).

St George's Hospital Charity is a registered charity (no. 241527).

Contents   page

Storyline

The following words are provided for readers or supporters who want to get some ideas about one possible storyline.

1. Ben is on a bus. It is crowded and noisy. A woman treads on Ben's toe. He feels stressed.

2. Ben gets off the bus. He looks a bit sad.

3. He opens his front door.

4. It's evening now. Ben relaxes with a cup of tea. He thinks about things.

5. Ben eats his breakfast. He likes porridge for breakfast.

6. He opens the door in his pyjamas. It's his support worker, Paul. Paul looks worried.

7. Paul points to his watch. But Ben offers him a hot drink.

8. Paul says it's time for the bus. Ben wants him to have a cup of tea with him. He wants to talk to him.

9. Ben looks upset. He is cross with Paul.

10. Ben throws his tea against the wall. The cup breaks – what a mess! Paul is shocked.

11. Paul looks angry now.

12. Paul says, "What's that for?" He looks bossy.

13. Ben pushes Paul – he is too close and too bossy!

14. Paul leaves quickly. Ben feels shocked. He feels angry and upset.

15. He sits in his chair and holds his head.

16. Then he thinks about Jane. He can ask her what to do.

17. Ben rings Jane.

18. "I pushed Paul," he says.

19. Jane comes to Ben's home. Ben is still in his pyjamas.

20. Ben explains everything. Jane listens carefully.

21. Paul comes back. Ben opens the door but he looks anxious. Paul looks worried too.

22. Ben explains. Jane and Paul listen.

23. Now Paul tells his story. Ben and Jane listen to him.

24. Ben says, "It's time to get dressed!" Jane looks pleased.

25. Paul thinks it's his fault. Jane reassures him.

26. Ben gets dressed, and Paul and Jane clear up.

27. Ben makes tea for everyone.

28. Jane shows Ben some pictures of different things to do. She asks Ben, "What do you want to do?"

29. Ben thinks about going out on a bike or to the gym; or going to the cinema or joining a book club.

30. Ben chooses cycling.

31. Paul likes this idea.

32. Paul and Ben shake hands. They both say sorry.

33. It's morning again. Ben wakes up. It's sunny outside.

34. Ben looks wide awake. He has a cycle helmet.

35. Paul arrives. He has a helmet, too.

36. Ben says, "Have a cup of tea."

37. They sit down together. Ben chats away.

38. Ben says, "It's time to get dressed!"

39. He pulls on his trousers.

40. There are two bikes in the hall. Paul puts his helmet on. They go out together.

41. Ben and Paul ride in the cycle lane. Ben is a good cyclist.

Feeling cross and sorting it out

We all know how it feels to get cross or lose our temper. Sometimes, when we lose our temper, we do things we wouldn't normally do. In Ben's case, he gets so cross that he ends up pushing his supporter Paul. Ben's story shows how, when Paul supports him in the right way, he feels relaxed and in control instead of cross and under pressure.

But the pictures don't cover all the ways to help people avoid feeling cross, nor do they show all the things people do when they lose their temper. For example, Ben's story shows how his supporter learns new ways of supporting him. While this can be enough, there are times when the person who gets cross needs to learn how to cope better with situations that make them angry.

The pictures in this book can help people think about the support a person needs to avoid them getting cross or upset or stressed. If this story is like your own story, you may want to work with your supporters or family carers to develop 'behaviour support strategies', and find better ways of dealing with difficult situations. Behaviour support strategies should always be part of an overall plan of support aimed at helping you to live your life to the full.

Ben's experience

Ben has a difficult time at the start of the story. He gets angry when his supporter asks him to do something he doesn't want to do. We all experience situations like this. And occasionally, when we get angry, we do things that make the situation worse – just like Ben, who gives his supporter a hard shove.

Sometimes, to avoid situations like this, people need to learn new ways of doing things. Ben's supporter learns how to help Ben express what he wants to do and how he wants to do it.

The following notes discuss this in more detail, and also give information on where to go for help.

What does good behaviour support look like?

The first step often involves family carers and supporters learning new and better ways of supporting you. This can include learning the best way to communicate with you, how to help you make choices and take control of your life, and how to support you to spend time doing the things that matter to you. In addition, it is often necessary to find specific ways of helping you avoid or cope with difficult situations.

No matter how hard we try to avoid difficult situations, there will be times in our lives when things happen that make us angry or upset or frightened. We might then respond in a way that makes the situation worse – for ourselves and the people around us. We may need to learn how to cope with difficult situations. For example, you may want to learn to deal with disappointments or having to wait for something, or you may want to learn how to tell someone that you want to be left alone, without losing your temper.

There are different ways of sorting out problems and learning new skills. In this story people talk very seriously about what has happened, but often humour can help you and your supporters to sort out a problem well, too. Sometimes reading or looking at pictures can help; sometimes we need to practise our coping and communication skills by 'role-playing' difficult situations.

Getting the right support

You can make a lot of things better by getting together with your family carers and supporters and working out the best way they can support you. However, you may also need help from a specialist, someone with the right training and experience who can help to develop a set of behaviour support strategies.

How to get specialist help

Social workers and GPs can help you get the support you need. Organisations like the Challenging Behaviour Foundation also offer helpful advice. See the Useful resources section (page 54) for a list of organisations to get in touch with.

What to expect from a specialist

A behaviour support specialist usually starts by finding out more about the difficult situations you have experienced and why you respond in the way you do. This will involve talking and spending time with you and the people close to you. They will then think about ways of making things better. This could mean improving the support you get from family carers and supporters, and helping you find new ways of expressing yourself and coping with difficult situations. The specialist will help you and your supporters learn and practise these new ways of doing things. Finally, over the weeks and months that follow, the specialist will check that things are working better.

Other people's stories about sorting it out

Chris

Chris was living in a house with six people, with staff support. He didn't get to do many of the things he liked to do, like having a nice chat with someone or going to the shops. He couldn't even make himself something to eat as the kitchen was usually locked. As a result, he spent most of his time wandering around with his head down.

Chris learned that hitting someone was the best way to get people to spend time with him. Unfortunately, it didn't just mean that his supporters spent time with him, they also used to hold Chris down on the ground if he hit someone.

The people who cared about Chris knew that he would be much happier if he lived in his own place with support. It took some time, but Chris eventually moved into his own bungalow. He also got a new team of supporters, and with the help of a behaviour specialist, they put in place strategies to improve Chris's quality of life and help with his specific behaviour support needs. These included:

- regularly spending time with Chris and always responding to his communication in a positive way

- supporting Chris to spend time doing the things he enjoyed, like going to the shops and making food

- leaving the area if Chris became upset, rather than trying to hold him down.

Chris no longer hits out at people. He regularly leaves the house to go to the shops or for a coffee. He visits his sister now, and goes on holiday every year. And if Chris wants something to eat, he just goes into the kitchen and makes it.

John

John struggled to form relationships with other people. This meant that he sometimes became angry and physically aggressive. He had been living with two other people in a house with staff support, but ended up being evicted because of his aggression.

A behaviour specialist carried out a functional behaviour assessment, which showed that John's relationship with his staff team was a big cause of his aggression. Other things that made him aggressive were demands and changes to his routine.

With this in mind, John started looking for a new place to live, and helped to choose his own staff.

A behaviour support programme was developed which included:

- a plan for developing good relationships with staff

- rules about communicating with John without making demands

- a weekly meeting with the service manager where John talked about any worries and helped to develop his own behaviour support strategies.

The situation got much better, to the point where John's aggression stopped completely. John now has far more control over his life and gets on very well with his supporters.

Helen

Helen found it very difficult to cope whenever she left the house. Being around people in the community made her very anxious, which meant that everyday activities like going to the shops were a problem. Helen could not speak, and instead used some Makaton signs to communicate. However, if she became anxious and wanted to go home, she would often attack her supporters or punch herself in the face.

A behaviour specialist taught Helen to use the Makaton sign for *finish* when she wanted to leave a situation she found stressful. Signing *finish* was a very useful skill as it made the same things happen as the behaviour Helen used before (for example, she got to leave the shop), but meant she had a safe alternative to hurting herself or other people.

The team made a list of all the community activities Helen found difficult, and then came up with strategies for each one. For example, to help Helen reach her goal of going into a shop and buying a banana, the behaviour specialist used a way of working called 'desensitization'. To begin with, Helen would stay in the car while a supporter bought the banana. Then Helen would get out of the car but stay close to it while the supporter went to the shop.

Over time, Helen got closer and closer to the shop, until finally she went in and bought her banana.

The behaviour specialist and Helen's team worked hard to give Helen the chance to try at least one new activity each month and learn the skills she needed along the way. As a result, Helen learnt lots of new skills, and her aggression and self-injury stopped completely.

Useful resources in the UK

Services

Community Learning Disability Teams (CLDTs)
These are specialist multidisciplinary health teams that support adults with learning disabilities and their families by assessment of their health needs and a range of clinical interventions. Teams may include therapists and psychologists, who can provide specialist intervention to support communication, activities of daily living, and mental health.

Dimensions
Dimensions is a specialist provider of a wide range of services for people with learning disabilities and people with autism. It is a not-for-profit organisation, offering support services to children and adults of all ages, including those with complex needs or behaviour that can challenge. See page 61 for more information.
www.dimensions-uk.org

Challenging Behaviour Foundation (CBF)
The CBF offers practical advice to families and professionals to help them support children and adults whose behaviour can challenge. Individual support is available by phone, email or face to face, and there are workshops on positive behaviour support and communication for families and professionals. A range of information on behaviour that challenges, health and caring is also available on the CBF website.
Support service: 0845 602 7885
support@thecbf.org.uk
www.challengingbehaviour.org.uk

Carers UK

Carers UK offers support to family carers with emotional aspects of caring for a loved one, as well as practical matters, such as financial support, Carers Assessments and respite.
Adviceline: 0808 808 7777
advice@carersuk.org
www.carersuk.org

British Institute of Learning Disabilities (BILD)

BILD advises on policy and produces a range of guidance on Positive Behaviour Support. This includes events, consultancy and training for schools and workforces. Training leads to a recognised national qualification in Supporting Individuals with Learning Disabilities.
www.bild.org.uk

Skills for Care

Skills for Care works with adult social care employers to improve skills and standards in the workforce and share best practice. A Workforce Development Fund is available for training support staff in various levels of vocational skills, including Supporting Individuals with Learning Disabilities.
www.skillsforcare.org.uk

Written Materials

The **Challenging Behaviour Foundation** produces factsheets and guides to all aspects of behaviour that can challenge, including *At-a-Glance Guides* for family carers looking for support for children, adolescents or adults. These guides are produced jointly with the **Social Care Institute for Excellence** and can be downloaded from the CBF website:
www.challengingbehaviour.org.uk/about-behaviour/at-a-glance.html

The CBF also produces a range of DVDs, including *An Introduction to Challenging Behaviour* and *Communication and Challenging Behaviour*, all of which are available free to family carers.

Supporting Me. A guide produced by **Southdown Housing Association** and **Skills for Care** for personal assistants supporting someone whose behaviour can challenge. This booklet covers ways to avoid incidents happening, through good communication and choice giving, as well as how to support someone well at each stage of an incident. The booklet can be downloaded from the Challenging Behaviour Foundation: www.challengingbehaviour.org.uk/learning-disability-files/Supporting-me.pdf

The **National Autistic Society** website offers information and advice on some of the specific things that may cause behavioural difficulties for people with autistic spectrum conditions, plus tips for supporting people well, and when and where to get help. www.autism.org.uk/living-with-autism/understanding-behaviour.aspx

Easy Guide to Physical Interventions. An easy read resource by **BILD** for people with learning disabilities, family carers and staff, dealing with physical restraint – 'strong holding'. The booklet covers types of restraint, safe guidelines and people's rights. It costs £7 and can be ordered from BILD: www.bild.org.uk/our-services/books/positive-behaviour-support/easy-guide-to-physical-interventions/

Related titles in the Books Beyond Words series

Ron's Feeling Blue (2011, 2nd edition) by Sheila Hollins, Roger Banks and Jenny Curran, illustrated by Beth Webb. Ron is depressed and has no interest in doing things. With the help of his GP and family he begins to feel better.

Sonia's Feeling Sad (2011) by Sheila Hollins and Roger Banks, illustrated by Lisa Kopper. Sonia is feeling so sad that she shuts herself off from her family and friends. She agrees to see a counsellor and gradually begins to feel better.

George Gets Smart (2001) by Sheila Hollins, Margaret Flynn and Philippa Russell, illustrated by Catherine Brighton. George's life changes when he learns how to keep clean and smart. People no longer avoid being with him and he enjoys the company of his workmates and friends.

Michelle Finds a Voice (1997) by Sheila Hollins and Sarah Barnett, illustrated by Denise Redmond. Michelle cannot speak and is unable to communicate her thoughts and feelings. She feels isolated and unhappy. Michelle and her carers try signing, symbols and electronic aids to find a solution that works.

Speaking Up for Myself (2002) by Sheila Hollins, Jackie Downer, Linette Farquarson and Oyepeju Raji, illustrated by Lisa Kopper. Having a learning disability and being from an ethnic minority group can make it hard to get good services. Natalie learns to fix problems by being assertive and getting help from someone she trusts.

Authors and artist

Sheila Hollins is Emeritus Professor of Psychiatry of Disability at St George's, University of London, and sits in the House of Lords. She is a past President of the Royal College of Psychiatrists and of the BMA. She is founding editor of Books Beyond Words and Executive Chair of Beyond Words, and a family carer for her son who has a learning disability.

Nick Barratt is a Board Certified Behaviour Analyst specialising in the field of learning disability and autism, with a particular emphasis on behaviour that challenges. Nick regularly presents at conferences on the topic of behaviour support and is part of a group of professionals and academics developing a set of competencies to guide the practice of Positive Behaviour Support. He also chairs a professionals' group called the Applied Behaviour Analysis Forum.

Beth Webb is an artist who helped to develop the concept of Books Beyond Words in its early days. She is also the author of fourteen novels for children and young people and is a professional storyteller.

Acknowledgments

We thank our editorial adviser Gary Butler.

We are grateful for the advice and support of our advisory group, which included representatives from Dimensions, the Challenging Behaviour Foundation, Respond, Betsi Cadwaladr University Health Board: Vivien Cooper, Noëlle Blackman, Margaret Flynn, Philippa Russell, Jane Williams, Nigel Hollins, Ron Harding, Peter Solomon, Fergus Carroll, Alan Powell, Clive Pressinger, Kim Stott, Alison Beezer.

We are also grateful to all the people who read earlier drafts of the picture story, including members of Bromley Speaking Up Group supported by Rachel Coates; the Therapeutic Support Service Books Beyond Words Group facilitated by Jane Williams, at Bryn Y Neuadd Hospital, Betsi Cadwaladr University Health Board; Researchnet Recovery Group at St George's University of London, facilitated by Paula Manners; and Aldingbourne Trust: Robert Chipchase, Kelly Marie Parry, Sandie Shenton, Dot Roberts, David Bliss, Edward Hamilton, David Stone, Sharon Packman, Holly Pace, Susan Smith, David Smith, Adam Southworth, Janet Foxon, Teresa Durman.

Finally we are very grateful to the Department of Health and Dimensions for providing financial support for this book.

Beyond Words: publications and training

Books Beyond Words will help family carers, support workers and professionals working with people who find pictures easier than words for understanding their world. A list of all Beyond Words publications, including Books Beyond Words titles, and where to buy them, can be found on our website:

www.booksbeyondwords.co.uk

Workshops about using Books Beyond Words are provided regularly in London, or can be arranged in other localities on request. Self-advocates are welcome. For information about forthcoming workshops see our website or contact us:

email: admin@booksbeyondwords.co.uk
tel: 020 8725 5512

Video clips showing our books being read are also on our website and YouTube channel: www.youtube.com/user/booksbeyondwords and on our DVD, *How to Use Books Beyond Words*.

Dimensions

Dimensions provides support services for people with learning disabilities and for people with autism. We aim to enable people to be part of their community and make their own choices and decisions about their life.

Many of the people we support have complex needs and some display behaviours that challenge. With the help of our Behaviour Support Team, we use a scientific, values-based approach called Positive Behaviour Support. Our partnership with Beyond Words was born out of a shared desire to promote support practices which are person-centred, respectful and based on an understanding of the interactional nature of behaviour that challenges.

A not-for-profit organisation, we are a leader in our sector, supporting around 3,500 people and their families in England and Wales, through a range of services including supported living, shared housing and residential care.

For more information visit our website:

www.dimensions-uk.org

How to read this book

There is no right or wrong way to read this book. Remember it is not necessary to be able to read the words.

1. Some people are not used to reading books. Start at the beginning and read the story in each picture. Encourage the reader to hold the book themselves and to turn the pages at their own pace.

2. Whether you are reading the book with one person or with a group, encourage them to tell the story in their own words. You will discover what each person thinks is happening, what they already know, and how they feel. You may think something different is happening in the pictures yourself, but that doesn't matter. Wait to see if their ideas change as the story develops. Don't challenge the reader(s) or suggest their ideas are wrong.

3. Some pictures may be more difficult to understand. It can help to prompt the people you are supporting, for example:

- Who do you think that is?
- What is happening?
- What is he or she doing now?
- How is he or she feeling?
- Do you feel like that? Has it happened to you/ your friend/ your family?

4. You don't have to read the whole book in one sitting. Allow people enough time to follow the pictures at their own pace.

5. Some people will not be able to follow the story, but they may be able to understand some of the pictures. Stay a little longer with the pictures that interest them.